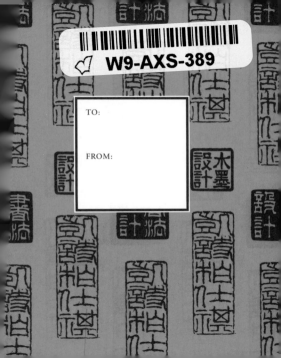

W9-AXS-389

TO:

FROM:

Illustrations copyright © 2000
Chris Paschke, licensed by
Wild Apple Licensing
Designed by Heather Zschock

Text copyright © 2000
Peter Pauper Press, Inc.
202 Mamaroneck Avenue
White Plains, NY 10601
ISBN 0-88088-333-2
Printed in China
14

Visit us at
www.peterpauper.com

FENG SHUI

The Art of Living

Feng Shui is an ancient and respected Chinese art, the essence of which is living in harmony with our surroundings. Our outer life reflects our inner life and hence, by creating the correct balance in our living environment, we create inner peace and improve the flow of energy in our daily lives.

This book presents simple tips that you can begin to implement immediately to bring the benefits of Feng Shui into your life. Mastering this venerable art takes many years of study, but here is a wonderful beginner's guide that you can dip into at any time and put to instant use.

Goldfish represent wealth and
fertility, and bring luck into
the home, but they should not
be placed in the kitchen
or bedroom.

The Chinese believe that a
solid front gate increases the
likelihood that your desires
will be fulfilled.

Get rid of clutter.

Hoarding creates stale energy.

Let it all go and trust the

process of life to bring what

you need into your life.

Spring clean those cupboards

and drawers today!

If your staircase is directly in line with the front door, hang wind chimes between the stairs and the door. This will moderate the manner in which the energy flows, so that nothing moves too quickly.

When furnishing your home,
remember that sharp corners
and angles create disruptive
energy and rounded objects
create harmony.

To create more movement in your life, replace still-life drawings and paintings with active art. For more ease and flow, replace geometric patterns with smooth-flowing works.

Refrain from hanging items
on the backs of doors. Doing
this increases the weight of the
door and adds more struggle
to your life.

Always ensure that your
bedroom is bathed in light.
Dimly-lit rooms full of
gloom create sluggish
and apathetic energy.

When positioning your bed,
ensure that your feet do not
point directly toward the door.
Energy enters rapidly, and this
powerful exposure may cause
sleepless nights. If you can't
move the bed, close the door.

Do not have your bed

directly under a window,

as this encourages you

to listen all night for

intruders and prevents

you from sleeping.

The electromagnetic fields that
emanate from a television
disrupt energy flow. If you must
keep a TV in the bedroom,
it should be shut away in a cabinet
so that the screen is not visible
when you sleep.

Place photographs of your children in rooms where people gather. This creates joy and shows the results of a happy union.

Household pets are most
effective in activating good
Feng Shui, as they are always
on the move, encouraging
energy to flow.

Battery-operated clocks and

radios are far healthier in

a bedroom, as they do not

emit electromagnetic fields,

which may cause stress.

When moving out of a home,

it is important to leave the

property as you would wish to

find it. This will promote

good karma.

A bowl of fruit on the

dining room table signifies

abundance, thereby creating

positive energy and

enhancing prosperity.

Your refrigerator should always
be full of food. An empty
refrigerator or pantry indicates
a lack of abundance. This also
relates to your love life.

Include rice in your basic diet.

It is an essential food and

provides supernatural

nourishment. Rice is

a symbol of abundance

and knowledge.

When pouring a cup of tea

for a guest, it is bad Feng Shui

to point the spout toward your

visitor. The spout sends out

hostile energy and can create

misunderstandings and

quarrels in relationships.

When you feel below par,

eat red peppers or tomatoes

and they will help to boost

your immune system.

Never serve tea or coffee
in chipped cups or serve
drinks in chipped glasses.
The Chinese believe that
chips and cracks cause
bad luck in business.

Waterfalls or fountains by the
entrance to your home bring
in positive energy. It is essential that the water is always
clean and flows continuously
to ensure purity of energy.

It is extremely important that the flow of the water in waterfalls or fountains be into and not out of the home. Water is directly linked to prosperity, so if water is flowing out, so is money, and vice versa.

Before taking a bath,

swish the water with your

hands to stimulate

the energy.

When spring cleaning,
add salt to the water in the
bucket or pail. Salt water
raises the energy levels
in your home.

Check that there are no
leaking faucets in your home.
They indicate money
flowing away from you.

To enhance financial prosperity,

always keep the toilet lid

down when not in use.

If the lid is up you risk flushing

your profits down the drain.

In addition, the bathroom door

should always remain closed.

The Chinese believe that a bowl of
holy water placed under the bed of a
child will help dispel nightmares.
Holy water can be made by
leaving water in a bowl out in sun
or moonlight for a period of time,
or it can come from a spring or well
that has been deemed to be holy.

Always keep windows

clean to ensure clarity

of vision in your life.

Avoid fluorescent lighting

in order to lower levels

of negative ions.

Keep mirrors framed

unless they are recessed.

Raw edges produce raw

edges in your life.

Cracked mirrors
in your home should be
removed, as they
fragment your life.

When positioning mirrors, do not place them to reflect each other. Energy will bounce around, going nowhere.

If a large mirror is not in use,

store it face down to avoid

energy emanations that

may cause chaos.

When working in your garden,

stop and savor the colors of

nature. Nature's colors have

great healing properties and

can soothe the mind.

Upward-shooting, rounded-leafed indoor plants increase the oxygen level and lift the energies in your home.

Put fresh flowers in your living room and workplace. Make sure that you throw them away as soon as they start to fade. Anything dead or decaying creates negative energy.

Do not have plants with thorns,
such as cacti, in the home.
They give out bad energy and may
cause arguments. Used out of
doors, however, they act as
protection against harm entering
your home or workplace.

Placing plants near your
computer equipment will
help to absorb the harmful
energies being emitted.

Avoid using dried flowers

in your home, as they

represent dead energy.

The color green will

reveal the path to new

growth and love.

Warm colors such as rose,

gold, and terra-cotta reflect

warm feelings and an

energetic and passionate

approach to life.

Cool colors such as
mint green and ice blue
represent calmer, more
passive energy.

Red creates passion and

promotes sexual bonding.

Pure white

enhances creativity.

The color purple is the most

spiritual of all colors.

Use gold for well-being

and for healing past hurts.

Blue is the color
of protection. It is a calm
and peaceful color that
encourages inspiration.

Clear out negative energy

in a room by burning

pure essential oils.

Before an important date,

burn neroli oil. This will

lift your spirits and

boost your confidence.

If you are coming down
with a bad cold, burn some
tea tree oil. It is a powerful
antiseptic and helps
fight infection.

Light candles and burn incense to enhance the flow of energy. (Always ensure that they are used at a safe distance from fabrics and pets, and out of the reach of small children.)

*Crystals enhance positive energy.
Their striking colors reflect light
beautifully, especially in a sunny
window. Before using and displaying
crystals, remove any negative energy
by soaking them in salt water.*

Amethyst reduces stress
and alleviates insomnia.

Rose quartz promotes balance.

Sapphire calms nerves and increases creativity.

Blue tourmaline releases blocked emotions.

Amber protects against taking on another's pain.

Hematite helps relieve stress during air travel.

Blue topaz calms body and mind and increases concentration.

Carnelian increases fertility and reduces menstrual problems.

Put a vase or bowl
of fresh flowers in the
bedroom of a sick person.
It will create positive energy
and speed recovery.

In order to improve your sleep, place a glass of water by the bed, level with your head. Do not drink the water, but throw it away the following morning. The water will absorb any negative energy while you are sleeping.

Try to include music in your daily life. Find the vibrations that relate best to your inner soul. These musical sounds will bring joy and banish any gloom or depression.

Treat yourself to some new underwear in pure cotton or silk. Synthetic fibers, especially nylon, create static and hold negative energy.

Make sure your clothes are
free from rips, tears,
or missing buttons. Being
badly-groomed is liable to
bring you bad luck.

When going for a job interview, avoid baggy, loose, unflattering clothes. They deplete your energy and cause you to become sloppy and uncentered. Garments that flatter your best features will strengthen your yang energy.

Wearing jewelry, especially gold and silver, creates an excellent balance. Being pure metals, they enhance your energy. Too much jewelry, however, creates an imbalance.

A pair of mandarin ducks

enhances your romantic life.

Lovebirds are the western

equivalent. Place them in pairs

to boost your love life.

Burning sandalwood oil
in the bedroom enhances
your love life. It acts as an
aphrodisiac and has strong
erotic properties.

Never place mirrors so that
they reflect you and your
partner in bed. The reflection
represents other people
intruding in your relationship.

Garnets help in matters
of love. Being red, they are
associated with heightened
emotions and arousal; they can
energize your sexuality.

Try to avoid sleeping with
a new partner in a bed shared
in a failed relationship. If you
cannot change the bed,
buy new linens.

To improve your love life,

bring some yellow into

the bedroom. It is a

stimulating color which

aids communication.